D0122290

i seen him when he done it

i
seen
him
when
he
done
it

a handbook on
Christian etiquette

by gladys blanchard muller
and
dorothy blanchard bennett

Van Kampen Press Wheaton, Illinois

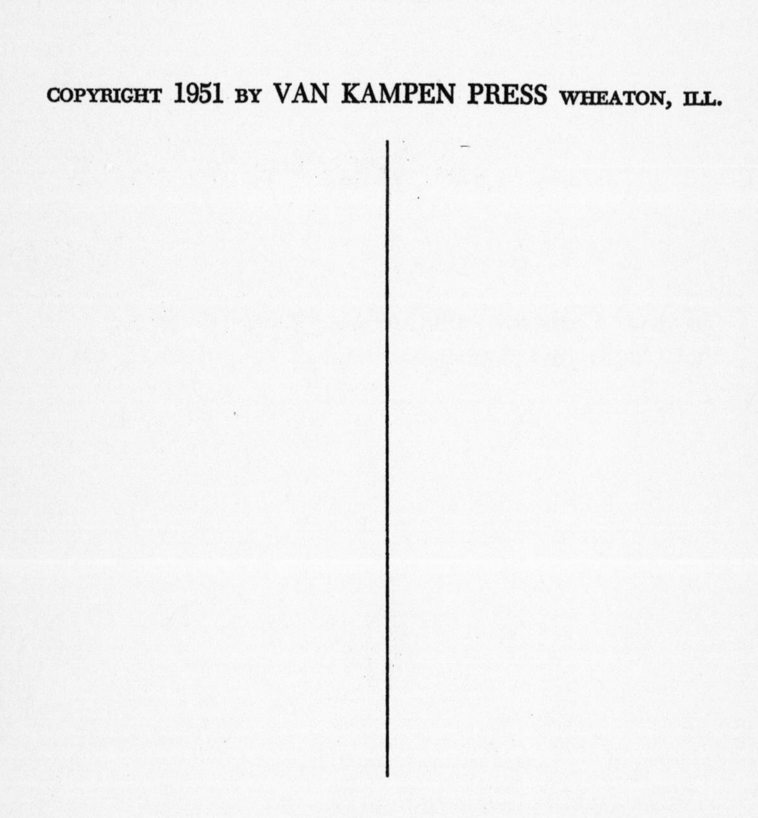

PRINTED IN THE UNITED STATES OF AMERICA

DEDICATED

To those Christians who are honest enough to see
their faults and courageous enough to put them away.

CONTENTS

My Neighbor's Bible

I am my neighbor's Bible,
He reads me when we meet;
Today he reads me in my home—
Tomorrow in the street.
He may a relative, or friend,
Or slight acquaintance be;
He may not even know my name,
Yet he is reading me.
And pray, who is this neighbor
Who reads me day by day,
To learn if I am living right,
And walking as I pray?
Oh, he is with me always,
To criticize or blame;
So worldly wise in his own eyes—
And "Sinner" is his name.
Dear Christian friends and brothers,
If we could only know
How faithfully the world records
Just what we do and say;
Oh, we would write our record plain,
And come in time to see
Our worldly neighbor won to Christ,
While reading you and me.

(*The Herald of Light*)

Let's Talk It Over

"I Seen Him When He Done It." What a peculiar title! No doubt this is in your mind as you begin to read this book, for it seems to be such a grammatical monstrosity. Most of us have become very sensitive to improper English and find it very annoying. But, are we as sensitive to the improper things that we do or the way in which they are done? Is this title any more disturbing than the rude, uncouth behavior we see practiced daily by many of God's children?

In a country where a King and Queen are in authority, great respect for the entire household is shown. Members of the family jealously protect the family name. You and I as Christians are members of the royal family of God; we are children of the King. Let us carefully guard our name "Christian" and behave as becomes our position.

This book has not been written as a manual on what to do and when to do it, for material along this line has already been published in books on etiquette which are available at bookshops and libraries. It has been written in a humorous style to stimulate thinking on a subject which otherwise might prove sensitive. Every attempt has been made to refrain from even a hint of sacrilege, and the criticism offered has been leveled not at people, but at practices which so often bring reproach on the work of Christ.

We hope that you will read this book with a smile, and yet prayerfully, as we seek through the printed page to present laxities that can easily be corrected by His help. May we pray like the little girl, "Dear God, make all bad people good and all good people nice."

This book had its real beginnings in the home of a minister, our father. From this vantage point we were able to see many of the bad habits practiced in Christian circles and the resultant damage, not only to the Christians themselves but also to those they were trying to win.

At A Church Service

God bless all those whose membership is here:
Thy people, Lord, who love Thy house and Thee.
And may we find in Thy great book at last,
Each name recorded for Eternity.

God bless the strangers gathered in our midst:
Lonely, perhaps, and far from home they need
The blessed comfort of their Father's house,
The proffered bread of life on which to feed.

God bless the one who here propounds Thy truths.
Be in his heart, speak through the words he speaks,
That every listening, eager one may find
The wisdom and the comfort that he seeks.

And when at last, the benediction said,
May we go, strengthened for the days ahead.

Grace Noll Crowell

WE GO TO CHURCH

(Congregational Offenses)

WHEN WE ENTER the sanctuary of God's house, how do we conduct ourselves? This seems useless to ask, but is it? Just the mere calling attention to these unlovely habits that so many have formed without thought will cause many to alter their ways, and by so doing make God's house one of holy quietness.

We go to church because we long to be fed on God's Word and to praise Him in prayer, song and testimony. Therefore, from the moment we enter the sanctuary we should be in the spirit of worship. We did not come to discuss the problems of daily life, clothes, raising of children—not even church activities. These things should not precede a service, as they tend to cool the spiritual warmth that silence can bring.

God's servant, if he is conscientious and desirous of seeing souls saved and Christians built up in the most holy faith, spends days of preparation and hours of prayer, that he might be a blessing in giving out the Word of God in a convincing manner. What he needs is our prayer help and undivided attention.

WHAT'S THE RUSH

One is not in the true spirit of worship when he comes

rushing into church, scarcely free from the odor of toast and coffee! An extra five minutes on Sunday morning may mean the difference between the whole family attending or the sending of a delegate. In these days of family disintegration it is refreshing to see entire families sitting together, instead of broken up categorically according to ages or interests.

Enter God's house in an attitude of prayer. Let nothing hinder this. It is inspiring to God's servant to see many of his congregation coming in, quietly seating themselves, and bowing their heads and hearts before God. This is his assurance that they are bearing him up before the Throne of Grace. These acts of prayer and reverence before the service are often responsible for inquiring souls after the service.

DON'T BE BACKWARD

Try sitting near the front: it's really the best place. You will find fewer hats to retrim and dresses to remodel! And even men will find it easier to concentrate on the sermon. Back seats should be used only for late comers and mothers with small children who may be forced to leave before the service is ended. The following chorus has been used with good results:

There's a seat in the front that's waiting for you,
Move up! Move up! Whatever you do;
The songs will be sweeter, the preaching will too,
Move up! Move up! There's a place here for you.

Taken from "I Sing of Thee"

DON'T MAKE A HAYSTACK OF YOURSELF

Are you a "Wilted Wilbur" who deposits yourself at the end of an empty pew, discouraging any but the bravest of souls from crawling over you? If you prefer an end seat, make it as easy as possible for others to enter the pew by rising to let them past. It is an alarming experience to be momentarily impaled by the knees of a Wilted Wilbur! Move in! The world pays a higher price for the center seats, and in most cases the Christians shun them. Why?

IS YOUR MIND A THREE-RING CIRCUS?

When our minds are filled with needless things before the service begins, the devil will see to it that these stay there, lodged securely and occupying our thoughts, thus keeping us from hearing and concentrating on His blessed Word. A sea of faces reflecting a lack of concentration has wrecked many a well-developed sermon, and it has become a reception of words and an utterance of congested thoughts. This can happen easily when God's servant feels the loss of attention from his audience.

THE NEWS ANALYST

Meet Calendar Carrie, the "gal" who insists on reading the bulletin during the service. How to control this is still a problem with the average pastor. Let's not be guilty of gathering our information while the service is being conducted. Church bulletins are not telegrams, and their contents do not require either immediate perusal or an answer. Do you enjoy talking to people who sit and read while you talk? Well, no minister does either!

DON'T BE A GRUEN GAZER!

Are you among those time-conscious individuals for whom, either consciously or unconsciously, the very phrase, "Dearly beloved, we are gathered etc.," is a signal to clock the message? One is seldom aware of the flight of time in an evening of social entertainment, but the "let's-get-going-spirit" reflected in the "what-time-is-it-look" can be seen on the congregational face long before the end of the usual ninety-minute church service. Heads pivot, seeking out the clock that some inconsiderate architect has placed at the rear of the auditorium under the balcony. Unable to locate the clock, or to believe its message, arms are raised full length, coat sleeves pushed back with a flourish, and the wrist watches given a thorough checking.

On second thought, perhaps that architect wasn't altogether inconsiderate! He may have had one of these pastors who lacked terminal facilities and needed a "timely" suggestion.

PURRING IN THE PEWS

Why is it that the first note of the offertory sets off a low undertone of muffled conversation in the congregation? Is not the offertory a part of the worship program, and the organist entitled to a listening ear?

"With all the purring in the pew
One can't blame the kittens, new,
For making noise and trouble too,
By copying what the old cats do!"

SUNDAY MANICURE

Hands are generally a barometer of general grooming. Well-cared-for nails are a sign of fastidiousness. However, the person who wields a nail file or knife and proceeds to indulge in the weekly manicure during the church service is nothing short of a pest! It is very agonizing to hear the rasping noise of a file, or to see one literally paring the ends of his nails while the choir drones, "Why Do You Wait, Dear Brother?"

If your nails have reached that stage where you feel they need immediate attention, have you tried biting them? Many seem to find this method most nutritious! But confidentially, close observers find it unsightly.

PERPETUAL MOTION

This is yet unrealized in the field of science, but gum-chewers have approximated it. The temples, ears, and mouth appear joined, and respond together with pulsating rhythm, turning the most beautiful or handsome profile into a carricature. Save gum for the privacy of your home! And as for your method of disposal—"Gum can be a gooey mess when tossed on the street with carelessness." Most people want rubber heels, but not gum soles!

GUILTY OR NOT GUILTY

There are several revolting habits to which many have fallen heir. One is that of tussling with the proboscis. That superword means nose. It seems to be a habit more prevalent among the male of the species and the young.

Germs Gratis

If your nose needs even the slightest attention, use that handkerchief—and don't check the results!

Another organ that seems to demand consideration as soon as the Doxology has been sung is the ear. With great dexterity a variety of tortuous implements are thrust into this hapless member, while everyone around registers disdain.

The last, but far from the least of these offending habits, is the pinching or toying with pimples. This sounds shockingly vulgar when it appears in print, but is much more nauseating when seen in public.

GERMS—GRATIS

Have you a cold? What are you doing for it? "Nothing," you say, "It hasn't done anything for me." But, maybe it is doing something in making you a poor neighbor in church. No one is to be criticized for bringing his cold to church with him, but the way he manipulates it is quite another thing. Sneezing, coughing, and blowing can all be reduced to a minimum of annoyance by using that handkerchief as a mute. Those around you are desirous of hearing the sermon and are not especially attracted to your brand or model of cold.

HYMNAL THUMPERS

Who are these folks? They are the ones who seem reluctant to hold the song books in their hands after the closing song, until the benediction has been pronounced. The books are dropped into the racks or tossed on the seats with such complete abandon that the minister often has to wait for the tumult to die down, or else forge ahead into his prayer, fortissimo.

Just listen next Sunday, and see whether your church group is guilty of this offense. If it is, maybe the correction can begin with you. Try holding that hymnal just a little longer. It ain't that heavy!

WALKER FAMILY

Almost every church has one of these charming little groups. They are the rather large family who straggle well down toward the front of the church on Sunday morning. By the time the special musical selection is given, Johnny is on his way up the aisle. When he returns, sister must go out. The whole service is taken up with the Walkers a-goin' and a-comin'.

Naturally there will be times when it will be necessary for a child to make a hasty retreat, but no one is disturbed by this. However, a well-organized family will take an inventory of its members' needs before the service begins, to prevent the occasional retirements from becoming habitual.

WHAT? NO HAT?

In this day of informal attire there is an increasing tendency on the part of many women to come to church without hats. The Roman Catholic Church requires women communicants to cover their heads, even if they must resort to the using of handkerchiefs or pieces of paper. Some of the more formalistic branches of the Protestant Church adhere to the same conviction, that the attire has a direct relationship to the attitude of worship. In many of our evangelical churches, our attempt to dispense with formalism has resulted in a general relaxation of those things which formerly created an attitude of worship. Surely it is no sin to come to God's house without a hat but, confidentially, isn't it much more refined to wear one?

SMALL FRY

There are times when the wee ones act as if they were hung on springs or seated on ant hills. There are many who seem to forget that they were young once, and found it difficult to sit within the confines of the pew. These individuals create more disturbance than the tiny offenders, by turning around to give the parents an "if-I-had-that-child look," followed by a dramatic sigh. Why not keep yours and the mother's blood pressure down by ignoring the noise? Should it be your lot to sit next to one of these jack-in-the-boxes, perhaps you will be able to contribute to his pleasure by producing some morsel of candy, a pencil, or some other trinket that will provide amusement. The news spreads quickly in juvenile circles about that nice lady or kind gentleman and, as an added attraction, the oldsters will "rise up and call you blessed."

PROPERTY DAMAGE

In the Old Testament we are continually reminded of the sanctification of the vessels used in the Temple. Have not the song books, pews, and other church property in this present day been dedicated to the service of the Lord?

Yet how many times we see song books carelessly torn, bent, or defaced in such a manner that one feels a sense of shame when they fall into the hands of visitors. Trains, bearded ladies, and even obscene poems often invade the covers of our hymnals. Names, monograms, and dates are etched on the backs of pews. Why must such a perverted form of art be expressed? Since the young are usually the ones so gifted with this talent, could not parents instill in their children an abhorrence for such sacrilege?

"WISE AS SERPENTS"

Inviting a soul to accept Christ as Saviour requires Holy Spirit-given tact. A person led by the Spirit to talk to the unsaved will do so in a quiet, loving manner that will encounter no embarrassment, because He will have prepared the heart. Unfortunately many sincere Christians have great zeal, but very little judgment, and by their careless approach have caused souls to either reject Christ or resort to false displays of decisions just to get rid of personal workers. Dealing with the unsaved is much more effectively done in a quiet place, away from confusion. If possible, take him to a room where you or someone else may open the Word of Life to him without interference or the stares of the crowd.

CLOSING CAPERS

The wise minister chooses a five-verse closing hymn for the convenience of large families. This provides ample time for the donning of galoshes, hats, coats, gloves and junior's snow suit. By the time the song is ended, they're all set to go!

In one of our churches recently, the minister's message had reached a very obvious conclusion. With dramatic sweep, he closed his Bible with force. This gesture was, to his hearers, a signal to start the dressing process. To the surprise of his audience, he smiled and said, "I guess I'd better open my Bible again. I see many people putting on their rubbers."

Do you think it must sadden the heart of our Lord to see how restless His children are in His presence?

DON'T BE A CYCLONE

Do you "blow" out of church as soon as the service is ended, as if the building were on fire? Unless that roast is burning in the oven at home, or little "sister" has escaped your grasp and is taking off her shoes and socks in the middle of the street, why not stay around longer? Welcome the strangers, be congenial; invite them to come again. Better yet, make it so pleasant they will want to come again. Your courtesy may mean the saving of a soul; your failure, its loss.

The Choir

ORGANIZATION FAUX PAS

THE CHOIR

ONE MINISTER referred to this organization as his War Department because of a continual state of battle among its members. Too often, singing in the choir becomes a popularity contest for personal aggrandizement rather than a service for the Lord. Take Queenie the quiver gal, for instance. Twenty-five years ago she aspired to become a lyric soprano, but found her pipes too flat. Time has not been too kind to her voice, but has not dimmed in the least her desire to be a soloist. She is crushed at the suggestion that someone else should be featured, but carries on bravely. Her metallic, quivering tones rise above the combined efforts of her loft-mates. Queenie is needed in the choir, but has never learned that the beauty of choral work is in the fusion of voices.

At the other end of the choir is Mrs. Low, an alto. She is attracted to this musical group because of her desire to be seen. Her wardrobe is extensive and bright. Sunday morning she really shines! Of course, this promotes a general feeling of good will.

In the back row sits Julius Pippydyke, the temperamental tenor. He finds it unnecessary and not always convenient to come to choir rehearsal, feeling confident that he will know the anthem anyway and will be able to anticipate the director's interpretation of it. The choice of music is seldom to his liking, and he feels it is his duty to discuss this with the other choir members who, up to this point, have been perfectly satisfied.

The choir is one of the important organizations of the church. Many hearts are prepared by its music for the message that follows. All service by the group should be done as unto the Lord, and every song rendered as though some soul's decision depended upon it. Here there should be true harmony musically and spiritually.

"What is it then? I will pray with the spirit, and I will pray with the understanding also: I will sing with the spirit, and I will sing with the understanding also" (I Cor. 14:15).

USHERS

Are ushers necessary? Why can't we come into church, find a seat unaided, locate the bulletins by ourselves, and regulate the ventilation without the help of an usher? We probably could, but the resultant chaos would scarcely be conducive to worship. The purpose of the ushers is to maintain an atmosphere of reverence throughout the entire service. There are many ways in which this is done.

First, the handshake at the door should reflect a warm and genuine welcome. Not the extended, limp hand that is slightly reminiscent of warm farina, nor yet the bone-crusher that buries the rings in your flesh. That firm grasp which denotes sincerity is the one we enjoy.

Along with the handshake comes that friendly smile that makes us feel wanted and glad that we came. Remember last week when Mr. Crabb, head usher, met you with that glum look, and you spent half of the service trying to decide whether you would offer him an apology (though you couldn't think what for) or a soda mint?

An alert usher will endeavor to seat people according to their needs. While it is true that many families occupy the same pews every week, there are always visitors whose choice of location should be ascertained in a quiet dignified manner. The older members of the congregation, whose eyesight or hearing is impaired, usually prefer to sit near the front. And, again, leave the back seats for late comers and families with small children.

Consider the attire of an usher. Obviously there is no standard garb, but a few "don'ts" are certainly in order. Even in the warmest weather coats should be worn while performing the duties of the office. It is disturbing enough to see an audience of coatless men, without those serving in prominent places falling into such careless habits.

Like all officers of the church, ushers should be chosen because they wish to serve the Lord rather than that they might be seen of men. A good motto for ushers is found in Colossians 3:17,23 and 24:

"And whatsoever ye do in word or deed, do all in the name of the Lord Jesus . . . and not unto men; knowing that of the Lord ye shall receive the reward of the inheritance: for ye serve the Lord Christ."

THE SUNDAY SCHOOL

No one will deny that reverence is befitting the Church at worship, but the Sunday School bell seems to change this to pandemonium. Why is it that a mere bell transforms children who have been cherubic during the morning service (and those who have been everything else but!) into screaming Apaches, warring on each other from behind pews, pursuing the enemy down aisles to the rear of the auditorium, where the now-combatant aged are trying to leave the church? These braves reach their Sunday School classes in the same wild spirit of play, to begin the study of God's Word. The result is that half of the lesson period is spent in calming them down.

Does all this commotion come from a lack of training in the home? Many times even adults have not had a vision of the Sunday School as the Church at study, and have been lax in impressing upon the young the need of reverence in this department.

Perhaps it would be well to explain to children the three spheres of church activity. Namely, the church at worship in the morning and evening service; the church at intercession in the prayer meeting; the church at study in the Sunday School.

DEAR TEACHER

How seriously do you take the job of teaching your Sunday School class? After the department superintendent has appropriated half (or more) of the period with songs, reports, and miscellany, what do you do with what is left?

Do you rehash quarterly material which has been hastily read with neither prayer nor reflection? The Sunday School lesson quarterlies were never meant to be the total source of material, but merely the patterns which stimulate the teacher's thinking. Poor indeed are both teacher and class where this condition exists.

It is also presumptuous of a teacher to face a class on the Lord's Day physically and mentally exhausted because of late Saturday night activities. While it may be fun and even occasionally necessary to indulge in these social times, be careful—it's habit-forming! The same goes for those facing the teacher.

Even in the best organized Sunday School it frequently becomes needful to use substitute teachers. All too often this process resembles the old game of "hot potato," with the unfortunate substitute teacher having a quarterly dropped in her hands at the beginning of opening exercises, while the superintendent flees down the hall, feeling he has done his duty. No wonder it is so hard to convince people to be on the substitute list. One does not feel very self-confident with fifteen minutes for preparation; nor does the class appreciate it either.

At best, all too little is alloted for actual study of God's Word in the Sunday School hour. For this reason organizational mechanics, such as the offering and roll call, should be dispensed with as early and rapidly as possible. And as for those Sunday School papers, may they rest in peace on a chair by the door to be distributed after the class period.

SAND IN THE GEARS

We are living in a highly organized age of bureaus, departments, committees, sub-committees, divisions, and commissions. This same method of carrying on affairs has filtered into the church, when we find the work divided among the various organizations. This is commendable, providing it serves as a means of delegating the authority to responsible persons, that the work of the Lord may be effective. No matter how efficiently geared, we often feel a resistance due to human faults, which are as sand in the gears.

Great care should be exercised in the choice of organizational leaders. The Scriptures have laid down some very personal attributes required of those in authority in the Church (I Tim. 3). Many times offices are taken because of the prestige and honor they give rather than the opportunities of service they present. Leaders should be chosen because of their consecration and ability rather than their popularity and bank account.

Then, take the Ladies' Aid Society, Here's a fine, well-meaning group of ambitious women! Our cousin, Sophanisba Bruinsmooge was once president of one of these organizations. But, lo, come the election day, and the votes blew the wrong way. She didn't even make one of the standing committees—so she became a sitting member (but not for long). The young upstart who had toppled her from the throne could never be capable of leading the Aid Society as successfully as she, and far be it from her to offer any help. The members found Cousin Sophie quiet and agin' everything in the meetings, but outside—not so quiet. The moral of this story—in serving the Lord, don't be a Sophie!

Many church officials look upon their tenure of office as they do on their marriages, "Till death us do part." This practice results in the stagnation of ideas and the under-development of potential leadership. No one is indispensable. Blessed indeed is the church with forethought enough to train its young people for organizational responsibilities.

Your Pastor and Mine

IF HE is young, he lacks experience; if his hair is gray, he is too old.

If he has five or six children, he has too many; if he has none, he is not setting a good example.

If his wife sings in the choir, she is forward; if she does not, she is not interested in her husband's work and is probably backslidden.

If he speaks from notes, he has canned sermons and is a bore; if extemporaneously, he is not deep enough.

If he suggests changes for improvement of the Church, he is a dictator; if he makes no suggestions, he is a figure-head.

If he makes use of illustrations, he does not give enough Bible; if not, his teaching is not clearly understood.

If he fails to please somebody, he is hurting the Church; if he tries to please everybody, he is a fool.

If he preaches the truth, he is insulting and meddling; if he does not preach it, he is a hyprocrite.

If he preaches an hour, he is tiresome; if only 20 minutes, he is lazy.

So what? They say the preacher has an easy time of it! Uh Huh!

Selected by G. R. Conrow
Used by permission

THE REV. AND HIS MRS.

OFT TIMES the call to the ministry appears as a call to a life of tranquility because of the prospect of association with people who call themselves Christian. Unfortunately this vision is soon altered by reality. Bickering, striving, the contention appear, bringing reproach not only upon the pastor and church but also upon the very cause of Christ. This condition is not attributable to the pulpit alone, but can often be traced to the pews. For this reason, perhaps an unbiased analysis of the wrongs on both sides might lead to possible correction.

Smiting The Shepherd

THE MESSY MESSENGER

When a minister stands in the pulpit he should realize that he is God's showcase, through whom the glories of the Lord are displayed. Many will say it is the message and not the messenger that counts but, humans that we are, the vehicle is still before us to attract or repulse. Neatness is not contingent on income. Hands that look as though they had overhauled the family car before service are very disconcerting when raised in prayer. Hair that reaches the Paderewski stage is not becoming in the pulpit.

Other menaces to platform dignity are the creasless trousers, unbuttoned coats, food-spotted ties, and unshined shoes.

"Certainly, this is a duty, not a sin. Cleanliness, is indeed, next to Godliness."—John Wesley

HE USES A CALENDAR INSTEAD OF A WATCH

No one would attempt to lay down a rule regarding the ideal length of sermons. However, it seems that there should be reasonable limitations within which a man can convey the subject to his hearers. Many a congregation follows its pastor only half-way through his sermon because the route becomes so devious, due to poor organization of material. "If you haven't struck oil after a half hour," said one seminary professor to his budding preachers, "You might just as well stop drilling."

MODERATO

Speaking of drilling, many voices from the pulpit have just that rasping quality. Some roar, in an effort to hold attention by their very noise. Others whine, emphasizing their sincerity in pleading tones. Still others, with naturally high-pitched voices, reach a crescendo. Each of these takes its toll on the audience in creating restlessness. A well-modulated voice should be the goal of every public speaker.

An old Kentucky mountaineer said, "We got a preacher that can holler a thunder storm back into the mountains."

A HAPPY MEDIUM

The matter of friendships is one to which the minister

and his wife should give great consideration. Many err, unknowingly. There are those who feel their calling demands that they remain aloof and detached from the personal relationships of the pastorate. They perform their duties admirably, but in a mechanical way that lacks the warmth required of confidantes. Then there are those who make a few friends, carefully chosen from the congregation, with whom they spend so much time that the others feel excluded. Their viewpoint becomes that of the few rather than the many. The green-eyed monster, Jealousy, stalks the aisles, accusing the members of the select groups or even the ministers themselves of "railroading" church policies. But those who are most likely to encounter real heartaches in this matter of friendship are those well-meaning servants who endeavor to break down all barriers. In their eagerness to eliminate reserve, they resort to a "big brother" form of behavior that calls members by first names, makes facetious remarks and indulges in other familiarities. In these and other ways they create unnaturally personal relationships that frequently "backfire." In a reciprocal manner, the parishioners feel free to dictate orders, call the pastor by first name, and in general show lack of respect.

Wise is the man who has found that it is the warm, friendly relationship to the whole group rather than to the few that brings the greater happiness to all concerned. He has found that it is more expedient to make his closer friends outside the confines of his church membership.

CONFIDENTIALLY

Because of his singular position in the church, the minister is the recipient of confidences, confessions, and even choice bits of gossip. Unfortunately these trusts often find their way out of the study, via the pastor's wife, or from the pulpit by unwise veiled references to recent interviews.

He that betrays a confidence is guilty of theft; he has given away that which was not his.

MADAM OF THE MANSE

Fortunately most ministers are blessed with mates who have felt the call as keenly as their husbands and, in spite of much criticism, have served faithfully. Some, however, finding it difficult to manage on the limited income common to the average pastor, have become disgruntled and embittered. They assume the martyr role, making continual references to their lack of funds and showing resentment to those who have more than they.

"The usual fortune of complaint is to excite contempt more than pity."—Samuel Johnson

HIS ROYAL HIGHNESS

Why is it some ministers feel that their positions entitle them to special privileges? You know the type. He hectors the baseball managers for special passes, the department stores for ecclesiastical discounts, and the car dealers for substantial reductions. He taps every available resource, both in and out of his congregation, for free merchandise. This same spirit carries over into his social life. When dining in a home, one has the feeling he has never eaten before and probably won't be eating again. His motto is "Get all I can. Can all I get!" This attitude does not befit a servant of God.

OLD ROCKING CHAIR'S GOTCHA!

Because a minister has no "boss" (except the Board of Deacons, Board of Trustees, the Consistory, and the Ladies' Aid!) to regulate his time, much depends upon the individual as to whether it is profitably spent. While many men work far beyond the "call of duty," there are those who do as little as they can. They have been known to make calls on the sick, if urgently requested, and even to visit the unsaved and newcomers when sufficient pressure was applied. Unless, however, one fell into one of these three catagories, he seldom saw the minister.

HEAP BIG SMOKE (And we hope)—NO FIRE

Perhaps no occupation presents such "reputational" hazards as the ministry. Because the pastor is often called as counselor in marital difficulties, he is placed in a precarious position. The frequent visits to the young widow, following the death of her husband, start many tongues awaggin'! Then there are those teen-agers with their attraction for "older" men, who make frequent stops at the church study for advice. All of these may be just "smoke," but you'll have to admit that many times there is a reasonable facsimile of fire underneath it all!

Most of these situations could be avoided by a little planning and forethought. To paraphrase the old saw, "You catch me once, shame on you. You catch me twice, shame on me." There are ways out of these trying situations. Take the "missus" along, especially when calling on those widows! Encourage the "sweet young things" to come to the parsonage study for counsel.

"Abstain from all appearance of evil" (I Thess. 5:22).

Flogging The Flock

Many of you have, no doubt, read the previous section addressed to the undershepherd with great glee, even emitting an occasional "amen" when faults of those servants were touched. Now, will you read, with equal open-mindedness, of the weaknesses of the flock? Perhaps if some of these were cleared, life in the church would be much sweeter.

DON'T EXPECT SOMETHING FOR NOTHING

Probably there is no more touchy subject in the entire field of church organization than that of pastor's salary. Many feel, with great conviction, that the minister is one called to his field and therefore, like the missionary, should "depend upon the Lord to provide." Their motto is, "We'll keep him poor, and the Lord will keep him humble." Yet these are the very folk who complain when the pastor's blue serge is shiny or his wife wears the same hat three years in a row. Oh yes, he must be able to dress well, donate to every charity, drive a decent car, and have an attractive home, so they won't be ashamed of him. They'll bring the water to the Lord, but if there's to be any wine, it will have to be by a miracle! Many a church expects its pastor to have the wisdom of an owl, the courage of an eagle, the enterprise of a jay, and the disposition of a dove, but they feed him like a canary. No man goes into the ministry for the financial returns, but the "laborer is worthy of his reward" (I Tim. 5:18).

DEFLATERS, INC.

Every church has a select few (and, we hope, they remain that way) whose chief aim in life is to keep the minister from getting a "big head." They feel that any praise should go to the Lord and not to man. It is dangerous to comment (except adversely) on his sermons or try his organizational ideas. Somewhere along the line they have lost the very real difference between flattery, which is insincere unwarranted praise, and a simple, honest appraisal of a man's work. For the older and more mature cleric these folks are—like Paul's "thorn in the flesh"—something to be borne with patience; but many a young and inexperienced man of God, having seen his ideas pricked like balloons and his sermons unappreciated, has fallen into the rut of despair, from which he has been unable to rise. Not satisfied with this masterpiece of deflation, these "select few" then complain that they have a lazy, unimaginative pastor. "Heaviness in the heart of man maketh it stoop: but a good word maketh it glad" (Prov. 12:25).

Right here a phantom choir chimes up, "But we don't want to change—what was good enough for our fathers is good enough for us. We've always done it this way etc,

etc." Whether we change or not, the world around us does. Some things become outmoded, while others remain as vital and effective as ever. We do well to be alert to the ideas of the young, and willing to at least give them an honest hearing.

THEY'RE HUMAN TOO

The classic phrase, "Water, water everywhere and not a drop to drink," uttered by a man on a raft afloat in the ocean, has its counterpart in the church. With activities by the score on every side, many pastors and their wives are "thirsty" for a purely informal meeting with their parishioners. They would prove happy additions to many social gatherings outside the church if given an invitation. You see, they're human too!

BETTER HIRE TWINS

The amount and diversity of work expected of the average minister is equal to the combined services of an economist, a politician, a fund-raiser, marital advisor, father confessor, disciplinarian, taxi driver, preacher, and pastor. He is expected to have endless resources of physical, mental, and spiritual strength available to his parish for their appropriation. He must always be enthusiastic about his work and full of optimistic fervor, even in the face of discouragement.

Since this pattern of expectations has been laid down, first by the pulpit committee and later carried on by the flock, it is not surprising that this "super" man is expected to visit all the sick and aged (as well as the healthy and young!), belong to civic clubs and take active part, teach a Sunday School class, direct young people's activities, and also prepare and deliver sermons fit for publication!

If this is what you expect of a minister, here is a timely suggestion: better hire twins!

MADAM X

No one objects to open, frank criticism that is given in a loving, kindly spirit. What every one hates is the note that is mailed from Kansas City (when you live in Ohio) and signed, "A Disgruntled Friend" (wrongly spelled—should be fiend!). If a matter is important enough to write about, it is important enough to give the recipient a fair chance for fight, instead of striking from ambush. "Brethren, if a man be overtaken in a fault, ye which are spiritual, restore such an one in the spirit of meekness; considering thyself, lest thou also be tempted" (Gal. 6:1).

THE WAY I HEARD IT

Gossip is the unnecessary passage of information (usually unverified) to others. Psalm 15:1-3 gives very definite teaching on this. If all news were judged by these two criteria, very little would be repeated. First, is it true? If not, why repeat a lie? Secondly, is it helpful? If not, why be deliberately destructive to someone? Gossip always harms at least two persons. We have taken the liberty to change one of Mr. Shakespeare's famous soliliquies on mercy;

Portraits of Preacher's Kids as Drawn by the Congregation

"The quality of gossip is not strained,
It droppeth, as the cruel hail from heaven above.
It is twice cursed; it curseth him that gives and him that takes."

THOSE POOR P.K.'S

Having spent the major portion of our lives in this catagory, the writers have very thin skins in this matter of the P. K.'s. Whenever preacher's kids do something disgustingly normal, the congregation wags its head and moans, "What more can you expect of a minister's child?" Considering the fact that these young ones are under constant scrutiny from the critical members of the church, and their deeds weighed on a different set of balances than used for others, it is not surprising that they are often "found wanting." It is no doubt true that these elements cause some P. K.'s to rebel and become real behavior problems; but this cannot be the universal result, for according to *Who's Who in America* more men listed in that publication were sons of clergymen than of men in any other profession.

Not only are the minister's children constantly under the microscopic gaze of the congregation, but the "old man" himself gets his share of inspection and weighing on the aforementioned balances. Others may be guilty of the same action; but when the minister does it, he is criticized. A critical spirit is like a disease that starts in an innocuous manner but, little by little, gains control of the whole person. It is also infectious and spreads to others.

The House Nobody Owns

Knowing how prevalent this fault is among Christians, we are quite sympathetic with the man who said that he was sick and tired of having "roast pastor" every Sunday noon for dinner.

THE HOUSE NOBODY OWNS

Part of the lure to a potential candidate which churches use to pad up an insufficient salary is the manse (or parsonage, if you prefer). The statement, "three thousand dollars a year AND MANSE" to the average church member is somewhat akin to giving the minister a salary plus a chateau in the Alps. Sadly enough, that chateau too often turns out to be a house of horrors. When built, the job was given to the lowest bidder or, worse yet, planned and constructed by well-meaning members after their regular working hours. Either way the result is about the same. Having been built, the property is promptly forgotten. Other homes in the neighborhood have an occasional facial, but not the parsonage. Weatherbeaten and forelorn it stands, year after year a symbol of deadlock between the minister, who can't afford to fix up church property, and the financial board who won't. Many a minister can say, "There's no place like home," without fear of contradiction.

Calamity Jane

OH, DOCTOR!

“ARE YOU a sickroom pest?”

“How could I be, when I am trying so hard to bring joy to shut-ins? Offend? Not I!” you reply.

“Well, someone does.”

“Who is this offender”, you ask.

Visiting hours are about to begin. The first harbingers of joy are arriving. Let’s see what they have to bring.

THE WOMAN WITH THE GRATE VOICE

She comes clacking down the hall, her heels beating a tatoo on the tile floor. Almost before she reaches room 522, she calls out her greeting in a loud raucous voice that resounds down the corridor. The patient, unable to retreat, must lie there and take it. There is little defense against a megaphone voice except to burrow deep into the pillow. If strength and courage would permit, under such circumstances one would doubtless find the patient under the covers with an “out to lunch” sign on the foot of the bed.

Remember—voices irritate or soothe.

CALAMITY JANE

This bundle of joy starts dispensing her black sunshine as soon as she enters the room with, “My dear, you look positively awful. Your color is bad, and you are nothing but skin and bones. Do you feel your doctor is giving you the proper care?" At this point the patient breaks out in a cold sweat. Insensitive to the patient's reaction, Jane continues, "Of course you'll need a long time to get over this, so don't be discouraged. Mrs. Soandso had the same illness, and it was several years before she felt like herelf again. And the hospital expense is so awful!" The patient weakly tries to offer some conversation, but gives up and feebly reaches for the bell to call the nurse. With the enthusiasm of a zealot, the visitor continues, "My, it's too bad you had to leave your children in the care of your Mother-in-law. I always feel that older people do not see the dangers that may befall children, but then I suppose you know what you are doing!"

With a shrug of her shoulders, Calamity Jane says she must be leaving lest she tire the patient! "Goodbye—I'll come again tomorrow," she says, as she passes the nurse in the doorway.

From the bed come a faint whisper, "Oh nurse, give me a hypo!"

SUNNY SUE

Our patient's next visitor is, fortunately, quite a contrast. Her cheery but quiet manner is restful to one so distraught by the previous caller. Sue has always been known for her originality in bringing useful but interesting gifts to the sick. Today, her bag of tricks contains a single flower that can be fondled by the patient, instead of being placed on the dresser twenty-five feet away. She also brought some light (both in content and weight) reading matter to while away the long hours, and to lead the mind into pleasant channels. Last week one of Sue's inspirations sent a beautician to the hospital to provide a manicure for her friend. The week before daily gifts, though unpretentious, arrived by mail.

"Sunny" brings to the sick room all the cheery news of events and people. She avoids subjects that cause worry or doubt to invade the mind that is already overly active from thoughts of unpaid bills, tasks unfinished, and loved ones needing her care.

As "Sunny" leaves the room she meets Dr. Goode, with nurse in tow, rushing in to give the hypo begged for earlier. Stopping short in the doorway, he is heard to remark, "Well, nurse, there is no need to give the hypo now. She's had better medicine—a cheerful visitor!"

THE BED-SITTER

This type of caller, when asked to have a seat says, "Oh, I'll just sit on the edge of the bed where I can be close to you." This is a thoughtless gesture. It not only causes undue motion of the bed, which may bring pain to the patient, but also tires his eyes, by placing objects too close. It might be more considerate to stand near the foot of the bed, where the patient has better perspective.

Don't be a sponger, let the fellow who is paying for the bed lie in it!

TRAPPED!

The church bulletin revealed that a man had not yet

accepted Christ, and for whom prayer had been previously solicited, was now seriously ill in a local hospital. Deacon Earnest, feeling obligated, rather than led of the Spirit, went immediately to call. He entered the room with an attitude of now-I've-got-you-where-I-want-you. The ailing one, sensing this, felt trapped and was antagonistic at once. The deacon made frequent references to death and the hereafter, endeavoring by this means to force a decision. After lengthy appeals and innumerable Scripture verses had been read, the patient, weary and confused, rebuked his caller with a gruff refusal. Even acceptances have been used to terminate lengthy visits!

Later the same day, Pastor Patience comes to call. His sympathy and understanding seemed to precede him. By eliciting from the patient some of his inner feelings, Pastor found how he might meet the spiritual need. A few well-chosen verses, showing the great love of God and His concern over the lost, began to make their impressions on this rejector.

"The word of God is quick, and powerful, and sharper than any two-edged sword . . . ." Without force, and yet with earnestness, the patient was brought to the place of decision and acceptance of Christ as Saviour.

REFLECTIONS

Conduct in a hospital while calling on the sick can cause favorable or unfavorable comment on the part of the hospital staff. Christian workers who are regularly engaged in hospital visitation should exercise care, especially on wards, that their conversations are confined to one patient at a time. The message when given in a loud voice may lose its effect by proving embarrassing to the one for whom it is intended, and may not be applicable to the one in the next bed.

The practice of dealing with nurses and doctors who are on duty is also open to question. Rather than engaging these busy people in time-consuming conversations, suitable Christian literature of an interesting, attention-getting nature, might be quietly given to them. These silent messengers, combined with a consistent testimony, will often bring the desired results.

TO THE UTTERMOST PARTS

It is doubtful that the command to "Pray without ceasing" was written to hospital visitants. There is a time and place for the longer prayer, but sick room etiquette does not include it. Pray briefly and to the point.

The story is told of a minister's calling on one of his parishioners who was seriously ill in a hospital. Before taking his leave, he said, "Shall we have a word of prayer?" He prayed for all people, all situations, and all the missionaries in various parts of the world. When the "amen" was said, he turned to the weeping relative beside him and said, "I hope your brother will soon be better." To his surprise she replied, "Oh, he died while you were in China."

Somebody gave a little tract
To a soul bound with despair,
The message gripped, the Spirit worked,
The Word had power, and we behold
A life released from Satan's snare.
    Was that Somebody you?

TIPS ON TRACTS

IN RECENT YEARS tract distribution has become one type of ministry that has been greatly used of the Lord. Because of its intrinsic nature many persons who are not formally trained for Christian work have been able to give out the Word of God through this channel. By means of tracts those with speech and hearing defects have been enabled to carry on an active ministry. However, because of its enormous scope and the numbers of people involved, much damage has been done to the cause of Christ due to careless distribution. The careful selection and prayerful sowing of the Word will break down some of the present antagonism which many feel against tracts. Not only is the seed itself important, but the manner in which it is sown is vital.

CHOOSING THE SEED

Tracts should be critically evaluated in considering them for distribution. Too often literature containing confusing statements or even fallacious doctrines is given out without first having been read.

The indiscriminate use of tracts has brought reproach. Pamphlets on the evils of the movies, card playing, tobacco, liquor, dancing, bobbed hair, and other forms of so-called "worldly pleasure," given to the man on the street accomplish little, as his need is for salvation. After this matter has been settled and the Spirit has convicted, perhaps these tracts may be used effectively.

Select tracts with eye appeal, the kind that arouse curiosity and interest. Those with catchy phrases, bold print, and clever pictorial presentations are especially attractive. Unsaved people will not struggle through cheaply printed, lengthy, and uninteresting bits of literature.

SHOP CAREFULLY FOR TRACTS

Choose the tract with a specific person or place where it will be used, in mind. There are tracts for all ages, professions, doctrines, and those touching on the various experiences of life. A tract entitled "Sunset of Life" has little effect on the sixteen-year-old. The effective choice of literature was recently shown when a friend placed a tract entitled, "What Do You Weigh?" on a scale in Syracuse, New York. The following day, when taking the Staten Island ferry from New York City, he noticed a Jewish man standing at the rail reading a similar tract. He turned to our friend and said, "This is very interesting. I found it on a scales in Syracuse yesterday." One never knows how far-reaching this ministry can be if done properly.

Don't forget the children. There are clever, fascinating, and interest-holding tracts for the young. The problems of adolescents are dealt with forcefully by this means.

To carry on an effective tract ministry one should have a variety of "seeds." This presents the problem of having the proper tract at the proper time. Before one prominent professional man went on a business trip, he made a mental note of the types of persons he would meet enroute, such as porters, brakemen, conductors, elevator operators, chambermaids, and waitresses. For each of these he had just the right tract. By means of a simple filing system in his brief case, he had them ready for immediate use.

A bountiful harvest will be in store for those who carefully choose the seed, recognizing the types of soil in which it will be sown.

METHODS OF SOWING

As important as the seed, the method of dispersion may determine its effectiveness. Many a tract has been antagonistically received because it was aimlessly given. Have you ever seen the person with a fist full of tracts standing on the street corner, conscientiously shoving one into the hands of each passerby, with an expression on his face that seemed to say, "Well, my duty is done. Now it is up to you"! One has the feeling that such an one has been chained to the corner hydrant until his allotment of tracts has been dispensed. After all, if this service springs from a willing heart, the countenance will reflect it.

The "road-block" type of distribution causes much animosity. The immovable individual who plants himself in the middle of a busy sidewalk, forcing people to go around him and impeding those package-laden shoppers in their rush for buses, is a menace to this ministry.

Some feel the necessity of leaving tracts in the place of tips when dining in restaurants, on the assumption that what the waitress needs is Christ, not money. However true that may be, one needs to analyze the effect such an

Tract Instead of a Tip

act has upon the waitress. Because of her disappointment at not being rewarded for her services, she is not likely to take kindly to the printed substitution. If one is not financially able to leave a tip, or feels opposed to the practice of tipping, it would probably be better not to leave a tract. When an adequate tip is left, the tract will doubtless find a more willing acceptance.

Many tracts have been torn up or thrown away due to unwise methods of distribution. If the person engaging in this ministry is led by the Holy Spirit, he will carry it on in a dignified manner, re-evaluating his methods constantly, lest he bring reproach upon the work.

ADVENTURES IN BAD EATING

BENJAMIN FRANKLIN once said, "One should eat to live, not live to eat"; but wasn't he overlooking other benefits that come from eating together? Mealtime should not be merely a gastronomic process, but rather a time of resting from labors and of fellowship with the family. It is also the place where new friends are made and old friendships strengthened. By the same token we sometimes experience disillusionment, when certain of those whom we hold in high esteem begin their capers. For instance,

GREAT EXPECTATIONS

Certainly as Christians we continue our regular practice of asking the blessing when dining out. It need not be done with ostentation, but in a quiet sincere manner. Having thus witnessed in this way, great care should be exercised over the conduct that follows. Insulting, unnecessary complaints, and curt remarks do not correspond to the bowed head that the waitress and other onlookers saw earlier in the meal.

THE HARPOONER

This is the character who is either so absorbed in conversation or so anxious to be served that he reaches full arm's length, jabbing his fork into bread or meat. Now this is a dangerous procedure. Another offender may be coming in for a landing from another direction. Have you ever heard of locked forks? Or, consider, the plight of the defenseless hand that may be innocently reaching for the same dish!

There is a very simple remedy for this in a four-word sentence, "Please pass the bread."

THE CUP CODDLER

To be eligible for this ignoble title one must place both elbows on the table, grasp the cup firmly in both hands, and stay in that position until the contents are drained. Some feel that great dignity is added by slightly divorcing the "pinkey" (in sophisticated circles called the little finger!) from the rest of the hand.

This pictures two transgressions of the laws of etiquette. First, elbows should never be on the table; and second, the cup is a transport vessel only, and not meant to be held aloft enroute to its destination. After each sip, this vessel returns to its dock!

THE DOVER BOYS AT DINNER

A couple of generations ago teen-agers were thrilled with the adventures of the Rover Boys. The characters of this age are the Dover Boys, the folks with the mixmaster tendencies. They stir their beverages so thoroughly that the cup's contents soon becomes a whirlpool that floods their saucers. Now, if it's a full saucer you want, this is one way to get it. But if your goal is sweetened or cooler coffee, relax! Take it easy!

The Gesticulator

The clan of the Dover Boys specializing in mashed potatoes are not content with the job done in the kitchen, but add their talents by stirring, beating and mixing the gravy into the "spuds" until the entire mass resembles plaster. With a shake of our heads, we simply say, "tsk, tsk, tsk."

HUMAN AMPLIFIER

This is the man who put "din" in dinner. From soup to desert, a series of slushing, crunching, gulping sounds is emitted. Horrible Homer contributes nothing in the way of conversation, but bolts his food noisily, keeping well ahead of all others at the table because of his intense concentration on the job at hand. If he expects another invitation from his hostess, he had better realize that she is entitled to more than a mere consumption of her food.

"Says the crowd who eats with Homer, dear
'His food is the nicest you'll ever hear' ".

THE GESTICULATOR

The deliberate, convincing person at your side who brandishes his knife or fork when he talks is one to be watched. One feels a sense of insecurity when too much activity starts. How shocking it would be if one should read in the morning Tribune, the headline, "WOMAN STABBED WITH FORK AT CHURCH SUPPER AS MAN DRIVES POINT HOME."

THE FOOD INHALER

He is usually the lethargic type that slumps over his

food and runs a shuttle service from plate to mouth. The speed with which the fork conveys the food is amazing. To be successful in the feat, the head is held not more than six or eight inches from the plate.

A close relative to the inhaler is the victual tosser, who carries the load on his fork to within three inches of the opening and then throws it. Result? Dry cleaning bill, $1.00!

FLATWARE FROLICS

A good sword swallower is a rare find in the entertainment world, but it is the unique dinner party that doesn't boast at least one pretender to this title. This dexterous creature conveys the food to his mouth by means of his knife, sinking the blade in well up to the handle. With horror, those around him await the possible results. The amazing thing is that these persons seldom sustain any injury themselves, but their friends experience quite a rise in blood pressure!

Another chap who keeps everyone tense at the table is the one who leaves the spoon in his cup while drinking his beverage. Ma' friend, this is not only unsightly, but dangerous!

THE HOD CARRIER

This energetic fellow loads his fork to overflowing and tries to hoist it to his mouth. Occasionally the fork actually arrives with most of the load, but more often part is lost enroute. When he is successful in maneuvering a forkful, it arrives to find the previous cargo not yet swallowed. But this presents no problem, for it can always be packed in, even if it takes a little strategy. At this point it wouldn't be advisable to have him say, "Boo!"

HAVE YOUR PALMS BREAD?

Instructions for accomplishing this antic? Place a whole slice of bread firmly in palm of left hand (if right handed). Now, with right hand, proceed to slather butter or jam with a strapping motion. Bread is then elevated to the mouth, a bite taken, and the remainder deposited on the table cloth, since there is seldom room on the plate for this size morsel. Efficiency experts tell us that quartering a slice of bread, and buttering it as it is eaten, is really the most practical method.

HOWDY DOODY!

History records that Sitting Bull died in 1890, but his counterpart lives on in the man who remains seated when he meets strangers. He does not realize that when women are present and it becomes necessary to introduce either a man or woman, he must rise. For some reason this social error appears more obvious in public eating places, but it is equally deplorable wherever introductions are made.

All this down-sitting and up-rising throws our modern Sitting Bull into confusion, but a trip to the library and one hour with Emily Post would transform him into a "Risin' Bison."

HOOVERING 'YER TEETH

This is the process used by that rugged individualist who

makes indelicate, clucking noises as he attempts, by suction, to dislodge particles of food from his teeth. If this method fails to produce the desired results, he resorts to a savage probing with finger nails or any pointed object that is handy. Oh, oh, your vulgarity is showing!

THE STACKER

This orderly, well-organized soul cannot stand to see food left on the plates, so he industriously mops up all the food remnants with a piece of bread. Having thus prepared the dishes he neatly stacks them according to size, pushes them to the middle of the table, folds his hands complacently, and awaits the next course. This helpful eager-beaver should let the waitress or hostess remove the dishes as she desires.

FLOTSAM

DURING THE writing of this book, several items have come to our attention which seem to defy all classification. These bits of miscellany have been, like jetsam, thrown overboard temporarily. However, we feel they may be too valuable to leave floating, and so have rescued them in definitive form for your perusal.

PETTY LARCENY—that form of robbery most commonly practiced by accompanists when they engage in that game called "stealing the show."

SONG LEADERS are those individuals who stand on the platform waving their arms while the congregation does as it pleases.

INCONSISTENCY is that attribute possessed by car owners, whose vehicles bear banners for Christ but who drive as though they belong to the devil.

TUNE—what most church pianos are not in.

CRASH—the noise made by communion cups landing back in the racks.

GRACIAS—Spanish for "thank you", a term seldom used in churches.

COMPLIMENTS—those inflationary remarks that, when given in profusion make you burst, but in moderation, lift.

RED—the facial color of the person who has just been the target of one of those clever facetious toastmasters at a church banquet.

GUEST SPEAKERS—are those victims who arrive unmet, uncertain where to go, and for whom no plans have been made as to room and board. They usually land with the lowest bidders at public auction in the morning service.

UNCONSCIOUS—is that state of mind in which church members tote song books home.

SUBSTANTIAL—the degree of reduction we make on other people's ideas.

FROSTING—the "goo" that covers a nasty, cutting remark.

LOST CAUSES—Best exemplified by the Superintendent trying to assemble even a corporal's guard to start the Sunday School session.

BELLOWING—the tone of voice which is not necessary for pastors to use in order to hold the attention of the congregation.

FRUSTRATION—the emotion experienced by the teacher standing before a Sunday School class (any age) trying to teach the lesson, while they carry on lengthy whispered conversations.

THIN—the thickness of some Christian's skins which makes them overly sensitive to casual remarks.

BREATH—that about which people talk, when it is bad.

HEAVENLY MINDED—that which so many Christians are so much of, they are of no earthly good.

PULPIT—a piece of furniture on the church platform upon which ministers drape themselves.

SECOND-HANDED—the condition in which onions are highly obnoxious.

MORNING SERVICE—that period of time in the week when Sunday School teachers study their lessons.

Myself

One day I looked at myself,
At the self that Christ can see;
I saw the person I am today
And the one I ought to be.

I saw how little I really pray,
How little I really do;
I saw the influence of my life—
How little of it was true!

I saw the bundle of faults and fears
I ought to lay on the shelf;
I had given a little bit to God,
But I hadn't given myself.

I came from seeing myself,
With the mind made up to be
The sort of a person that Christ can use
With a heart He may always see.

Author unknown

I SAW HIM AND HE DIDN'T DO IT

IT WOULD not be surprising if there were many varied reactions to this book. Some have felt that the matters written about here might better have been ignored. Time has shown, however, that correction of wrong is not accomplished by disregarding it. Other readers may have been irritated or piqued. They are the ones whom the "shoes have fit", and they are angry at the pinch. There is a possibility that even they, as time goes by, may shed some of these unlovely habits because they have become conscious of them. We hope, however, that to the greater number the book has been a source, not only of amusement, but of real evaluation and resolution. It is to these courageous souls the book is dedicated.

Having seen some of the shortcomings prevalent among Christians that ofttimes become stumbling blocks to the unsaved, we should feel impelled to mend our ways. We are prone to put up umbrellas of self-righteousness when the rain of criticism comes. It hits everyone but us. A frankly critical examination of self must come first. Such insight should create in us the desire to remove these unlovely practices (Prov. 28:13). We are enabled by the Holy Spirit to accomplish this.

Groups of Christians gathered for fellowship, might find it helpful to talk over these offenses which do not befit us as children of God. While great care must always be taken in these discussions that personalities are not attacked, group thinking strengthens convictions which bring about change in individual behavior.

Many of these faults would never have been born had parents lived and taught Christian courtesy in the home. As the Scriptures are read at the family altar and prayers are made for daily guidance, there is bound to be a growing sensitivity to "the sins that do so easily beset us." One cannot divorce his Christian testimony from his daily behavior.

"I SEEN HIM WHEN HE DONE IT?"

"NO!"

"I SAW HIM AND HE DIDN'T DO IT!"